# The Power of God Prevails Over You

Bishop K. R. Simmons

Copyright © 2014 Bishop K. R. Simmons

All rights reserved. No part of this book may be reproduced in any form or by any means, electronic or mechanical, including photo-copying, recording, or by any information storage and retrieval system, without written permission from the author. This excludes a reviewer who may quote brief passages in a review.

Unless otherwise noted, all Scripture quotations are from The Holy Bible, King James Version (KJV)

Cover Design: Brittany J. Jackson

Published by G Publishing, LLC

ISBN: 978-0-9971579-4-9

Printed in the United States of America

# Table of Contents

Introduction .......................................................7

Chapter One: The Power of God Prevails over your Mind........................................................12

   Praise and Worship: Mind Connecting Ingredient......................................................18

Chapter 2: The Power of God Prevails Over Your Body ........................................................23

   Prayer of Salvation ......................................31

Chapter 3: A Life Ablaze with the Power of God and the Holy Spirit ..................................33

   Study Scriptures on the Holy Spirit............41

About the Author.............................................43

Something Wonderful is going to Happen to You!

It is Predestined by God!

# Introduction

God is a prevailing predominant and immediate spirit to the born again believer. He has superior force and influence over our lives. As a born again believer, baptized and infiltrated by the power of the Holy Spirit and the anointing. You have the supernatural ability and protection that the enemy cannot penetrate. As a specialist in the art of deception, deceit, and un-told truths, the enemy will attempt to overtake you and destroy you in many ways. One of the ways he attempts to overtake and destroy you is through your mind. Your mind is the forerunner and leader of your actions, (Proverbs 23:7). For as he thinketh in his heart, so is he….? A negative mind produces negative thoughts. A positive thinking mind is necessary and vital to the success of a born again believer. It is a mind running over with thoughts of faith and life of victory over the enemy. Another method that the enemy will try to use to defeat you in your walk with the eternal God is sickness to your body, this is an indisposed spirit. If the enemy can just wage war against organs in your body, it will hinder your belief system; birthing in you a spirit of doubt, fear and unbelief. This is what I call the ingredients that make up the devil faith. God's word is spoken of in proverbs 4:22, (As being medicine to all our flesh." It is the most powerful medicine available today, and it is capable of healing your body without side effects. Our confession of the word of God calls for healing which is already ours. So speak the powerful words of God to the sickness in your body and then prepare yourselves to receive your sighs, wonders, and miracles in the name of Jesus Christ of Nazareth. Then tell that sickness demon to vacate your body immediately, without delay.

Finally, the enemy will wage an all out attack against your spirit man. First off beloved, the spirit is the source of spiritual life. Secondly, it is the source of spiritual overflow. That is apparent in John 7:37-39, where Jesus says, "If anyone is thirsty, let him come to me and drink, whoever believe in me, as the scripture has said, streams of living water will flow within him." By this, He meant the spirit, whom those who believed in Him were later to receive. Up to that time the spirit had not been given, since Jesus had not yet been glorified. While Jesus emphasized the spirit's inflow in John 3, He emphasizes the spirit's outflow in John 7. Beloved, as a born again believer and Christian, we all should be filled with the spirit so that we have not only grace for our own needs, but an overflowing grace for others. Satan is always endeavoring to bring the people of God into disrepute, but the Holy Spirit never comes with condemnation. He always brings us help. The Lord Jesus referred to Him as the comforter who would come. He is always on hand to help in the seasons of trial and test.

The Holy Spirit is the lifting power of the church. Paul tells us that we are manifestly declared to be the epistle of Christ written not with ink, but with the spirit of the living God; not in tables of stone, but in fleshy tables of the heart. The Holy Spirit begins in the heart, right in the depths of human affections. He brings into the heart the riches of the revelation of Christ, implanting purity and holiness there. This means out of the depths of your heart, praises may rise up continually. When we live in the spirit, the old allurements have lost their power. The devil will meet you at every turn, but the spirit of God will always "lift up a standard against him."

In conclusion, beloved, we must come to the end of ourselves so the spirit may work without hindrance in our lives. Self-will and self-interest are the great enemies of the spirit in the life of a believer. Cleansing from these by the spirit, frees us to be acceptable instruments of His grace. Oh, that all of us who bear His word would not only let the Spirit give new life through new birth, but also cleanse our spirits until we are emptied of self-interest so that He reigns within! Effective Christian living and serving begins with Christ's provision for us His spirit.

# Chapter One: The Power of God Prevails over your Mind

It was once penned by one of God's great orators of the Gospel, "Life is always composed of those experiences and encounters which provide both challenges to one's character and the testing of one's spirit. Life's greatest wars are never waged on plains of mortal combat and or physical struggles. Life's greatest wars are fought on the <u>battlefield of the mind</u> Life's most serious conflict is inner conflict, and the scars of war that inflict the most permanent wound and causes the greatest pain are to be found not on the skin, but on the soul and in your mind. From scripture, we see we are at war. "For we are not wrestling with flesh and blood, but against the powers against the world rulers of the present darkness, against the spirit forces of wickedness in the heavenly sphere." (Ephesians 6:12).

Beloved we are under attack by the enemy (devil). He is relentless in his endeavors to subdue you in your mind and win. The weapon the enemy (devil) uses is the weapons of doubt, worry, confusion, fear and depression. When one operates in a lifestyle of any of the previous mentioned characteristics of the enemy (devil), it will diminish your ability to have faith for signs, wonders and miracles. Without faith, the bible tells us it is impossible to please God. The lack of faith ties God's hands of blessing to you. God moves out in faith of the born again believer. Faith in God is the most power force known to man. A great writer once penned, "Faith is a means by which you can put yourself in a frame of mind to tune in and draw upon the universe." God is that power. You as a born again believe in God. You have a right to tap into the reservoir of

God's blessings for your life. The blessings of signs, wonders and miracles. As the carpenter from the plains of Galilee said, "According to your faith, so be it unto you."

So many Christians today experience spiritual warfare in their minds. The enemy (devil) finds this area of the human anatomy be a prime target of his deceitful attempt destroy you with his plans that are especially laid out and extremely dangerous to the born again believer. The enemy knows if he (devil) can infiltrate your brain, which is the covering of your mind. This is the portion of the central nervous system in the vertebrate cranium that is responsible for the interpretation of sensory impulses, the coordination and control of bodily activities, and the exercise of emotion and thought. If he (devil) can setup strongholds in your head of spiritual defeat, it would destroy the existence of the spirit man that resides in you. If the spirit man is allowed to die in you, it would be a perilous outcome in the born again believer. You would be in a state of powerlessness and hopelessness with no spiritual direction. The spiritual wisdom in you is no longer operative because of the murderous deeds of the enemy.

We, as born again believers, must not allow the enemy to set up strongholds in our minds. It is so very important that our minds be filled with the word of God. It is the power of the Holy Spirit working through the word of God that brings victory into our lives when faced with the trickery of the enemy. We must keep the powerful word of God in us for mind renewing power. In doing so, it enables us to tear down stronghold attacks against our mind by the vain attempt of the enemy (devil). For it is written in 2 Corinthians 10:4-5, ". . . to tear down strongholds and every high and lofty thing exalts itself against the word of God . . ." It is the word of God living and sweltering inside of us that allows us to be strengthen for spiritual progress. God wants us to be victorious born again believers. This is why it is so important for us to have a transformation renewed mind. ". . . Do not be conformed to this world, but be transformed by the renewal of your mind so that you may prove what is the good and perfect Will of God, even the thing which is good and acceptable in His sight for you." (Romans 12:2)

Apostle Paul is saying to us a renewed, transformed mind will bless one to see God's good and perfect will in their life. Beloved having the mind of Christ operating in us is so necessary for continued growth in Christians and a life of continuous victories over the enemy (devil). ". . . But we have the mind of Christ and do hold the thoughts of His heart." (1 Corinthians 2:16). Beloved, when we have the mind of Christ operating in us, the enemy will aggressively stand against the renewal process of your mind. Be determined. A continual affirmation of God's word in faith will build into your spirit man a supernatural anointing that is capable of eliminating the enemy (devil) attack against your mind. Jesus said "If ye abide in me, and my words abide in you, ye shall ask what ye will and it shall be done unto you"(John 15:7). When God's word becomes engrafted or infused into your spirit it has become a part of you. It cannot be separated from you. It is not only your thought and affirmation. It is you! The word made flesh. Then your flesh will reflect the life of that word. When God's word takes root in you, it becomes greater than the enemy (devil). You have what it takes to fight the good fight of faith. Be obedient to the word of God. It was once said, "Obedience is a far-reaching thing. It closes the gates of hell and opens the windows of heaven." "For as by one man's disobedience many were made sinners, so by the obedience of one shall many be made righteous." (Romans 5:19). Beloved, our minds must be filled with all the fullness of God. His word must be connected to our minds and our minds to it. Then we will see the evidence of signs, wonders, and miracles operating in every facet of our lives.

## Praise and Worship: Mind Connecting Ingredient

Praise and Worship is a connecting point to which our mind and thoughts can be lined up with His (God) thoughts of revelation to us and His (God) presents. It is penned in the word of God that God inhabits the praises of his people and where ever God is, there is a blessed assurance and a foretaste of heaven. Where ever God is, sin-sick souls can find Jeremiah's balm in

Gilead. Struggling spirits can find the higher ground of heaven's table land. Where ever God is, the disturbed and the distraught can escape the sinking, shifting sands of a crumbling culture and stand on solid rock. The alienated and the frustrated can find a faith where there is nothing between the soul and the savior. Where ever God is, there is an abiding confidence present, a vital and necessary supernatural power and anointing where the born again believer can connect with the peace of God which passes all human knowledge and intelligence. It is a place in His presence where a born again believer can shut - out and shed-in. Shut-out those things that try to hinder you from being in His presence.

Doubt is one key factor in blocking your entrance to His presence. The enemy (devil) would like to rob you of every blessing God has for you. Disbelief, fear, worry and confusion are all mixed up with doubt. Do not allow doubt to invade your conversation or into your heart. Shut it out of your mind. Trust God. The bible says in Ephesians 3:20, "Now unto Him that is able to do exceeding abundantly above all that we ask or think, according to the power that worketh in us." That power is evident when we shut ourselves into a place of praise and worship it allows us to meet God at the very point of our needs. When we, as born again believers, shut-in to the presence of God through praise and worship, in doing so, God gives power to the faint and to them that have no might. He increases strength. When we shut-into the presence of God, no need to toss and turn and have sleepless nights. No need for one to walk back and forth pacing holes in their carpets. When one shut-in to His presence, the power of God prevails. He is in charge. God has power to alter men, nations and nature.

As a born again believer, we have the promise of His presence through power of praise and worship. I just want to reassert and reaffirm the importance of this spiritual divine mandate to born again believers. Praise and worship is not just for Sunday morning church services and/or weekly prayer meetings. True praise and worship must be a way of life for the born again believer.

When we praise and worship God, life struggles are taken away. It allows us to be able to rest and be at peace. This is total mind surrendering and concentration on God. This is how we as born again believers can see the evidence of <u>signs</u>, <u>wonders</u> and <u>miracles</u> in our lives daily.

Beloved, put this in your spirit: <u>Praise plus Worship equals Victory!</u> Remember the power of God prevails over you! "Trust in the Lord with all your heart and lean not on your own understanding; in all your ways acknowledge Him and He will make your paths straight." (Proverbs 3:5).

"Blessed are those who have learned to acclaim you, who walk in the light of your presence, O Lord." (Psalms 89:15).

"For I know the plans I have for you," declares the Lord. "Plans to prosper you and not to harm you. Plans to give you hope and a future. Something wonderful is going to happen to you!" Jeremiah 29:11.

# Chapter 2: The Power of God Prevails Over Your Body

"Do you not know that your body is a temple of the Holy Spirit, who is in you, whom you have received from God? You are not your own: you were bought at a Price." (1 Corinthians 6:19-20). (Today's light Bible)

Beloved, one of the most deplorable effects of the original apostasy was the loss of man's power of self-control. Only as this power is regained can there be real progress. The body is the only medium through which the mind and the soul are developed for the up building of character. Hence it is that the adversary of souls directs his temptation to the enfeebling and degrading of the physical powers. The tendencies of our physical nature, unless under the dominion of God, will surely work ruin and death.

The body is to be brought into subjection onto God. The higher power of the being are to rule. The passions are to be controlled by the will, which is itself to be under the control of God. The kingly power of reason, sanctified by divine grace, is to bear sway in our lives. The requirements of God must be brought home to the conscience. Men and women must be awakened to the duty of self-mastery, the need of purity, freedom from every depraving appetite and defiling habit. They need to be impressed with the fact that all their powers of mind and body are the gift of God and are to be preserved in the best possible condition for His service. In that ancient ritual which was the gospel in symbol, no blemished offering could be brought to God's altar. The sacrifice that was to represent Christ must be spotless. The word of God points to this as an illustration of what God's children are to be, a living sacrifice, holy and without blemish, well-pleasing to God.

Beloved, apart from God's divine power, no genuine reform can be effective. Human barriers against natural and cultivated tendencies are but as the sandbank against the torrent. Not until the life of Christ becomes a vitalizing power in our lives can we resist the temptations that assail us from within and from without. Christ came to this world and lived the law of God, that man might have perfect mastery over the natural inclinations which corrupt the soul. God, the physician of the soul and body. He gives victory over warring lusts. God has provided every facility that man may possess completeness of character. When one surrenders to Christ, the mind is brought under the control of the law, but it is the royal law which proclaims liberty to every captive. By becoming one with Christ, man is made free. Subjection to the will of

Christ means restoration to perfect woman and manhood. Obedience to God is liberty from the thralldom of sin, deliverance from human passion and impulse. Man may stand conqueror of himself, conqueror of his own inclinations, conqueror of principalities and powers, and the rulers of the darkness of this world and of spiritual wickedness in high places. (Ephesians 6:12)

Beloved, God has created you for His glory and purpose. Only He alone can move you to a place of destiny. God is omnipotent. This means He is full of power. The bible says besides him there is no other. God is El Shaddai, God Almighty. We must recognize God's supremacy. When Christ was about to give the commission to His apostles to go forth and evangelize the nations, He emphasized to them that mighty assurance of His Almightiness and Omnipresence.

"All authority in heaven and on earth has been given to me . . . And surely I am with you always, to the very end of the age." (Matthew 28:18, 20). This is beloved the warrant for our boldest faith, for our loftiest endeavor, for our most difficult undertaking. God sovereignty and supremacy are the supply of all our needs. Beloved the more we become less, the more He becomes greater. The more miracles, signs and wonders will overtake us. The more we die to ourselves, the more room we have to receive Him in His fullness. Beloved, we must understand it is not about us, it's about God. We live in an age of human self-sufficiency. When boasting, mankind is saying, "Come, let us build ourselves a city with a tower that reaches the heavens" (Genesis 11:4), and God is saying in divine pity and scorn, "Come, let us go down and confuse their language" (Genesis 11:7).

Beloved, once again, it's not about us, it's about God. It was once penned by a great orator of the gospel, "God is not just the starting point of your life, He is the source of it. Without God, life makes no sense. It is about becoming what God created you to be. Beloved, "A life devoted to things is a dead life, a stump; a God-shaped life is a flourishing tree" (Proverbs 11:28).

Blessed are those who trust in the Lord . . . they are like trees planted along a riverbank, with roots that reach deep into the water. Such trees are not bothered by the heat or worried by long months of drought. Their leaves stay green, and they go right on producing delicious fruit. (Jeremiah 17:7-8). It is catastrophe that many people die before they reach their destiny in God. They did not totally relinquish themselves to God and His plans for their lives. By destroying our relationship with God, it puts a cap on our destiny that God had planned for our lives. "What should have been." There is no limit to the usefulness of one who, putting self aside, make room for the working of the Holy Spirit upon his heart and lives a life wholly consecrated to God. All who consecrate the body, soul and spirit to His service will be constantly receiving a new endowment of physical, mental and spiritual power. To everyone who offers himself to the Lord for service, withholding nothing, is given power for the attainment of measureless results. For these, God will do great things. He will work upon the minds of men so that even in this world, there shall be seen in their lives a fulfillment of the promise of the future state.

(Romans 8:11) And, if the spirit of him who raised Jesus from the dead is living in you, He who raised Christ from the dead will also give life to your mortal bodies through His spirit who lives in you.

Beloved, it was once penned by a famous writer, "What lies behind us and what lies before us are tiny matters compared to what lies within us. Beloved, let the power of God take full control of your body, that you may live a life of victory over the enemy. God created you to rule over all the earth and everything that creeps in it. He will never demand anything of you He didn't already build into you. Therefore, if the enemy has dominated you, you are living beneath your privilege and spiritual power that God has sanctioned unto you. We are led by the spirit of God; we are not led by our bodies. We don't determine whether or not God is speaking to us by how we feel. Our bodies are not a safe guide to understanding how God is speaking to us or how we are being led by Him.

"Therefore, brethren, we are debtors, not to the flesh, to live after the flesh, for if ye live after the flesh, ye shall die, but if ye, through the spirit do mortify the deeds of the body, ye shall live. For as many as are led by the spirit of God, they are the sons of God.

Prayer of Salvation

A born-again, committed relationship with God is the key to victorious life. Jesus laid down His life and rose again so that we could spend eternity with Him in heaven and experience His absolute best on earth. If you would like to receive Jesus into your life in order to become born again, pray this prayer from your heart:

*Heavenly father, I come to you admitting that I am a sinner. Right now, I choose to turn away from sin and I ask you to cleanse me of all unrighteousness. I believe that your son Jesus died on the cross to take away my sins. I also believe that he rose again from the dead so that I might be justified and made righteous through faith in Him. I call upon the name of Jesus Christ to be the Savior and Lord of my life. Jesus, I choose to follow you and ask that you fill me with the power of the Holy Spirit. I declare that right now. I am a child of God. I am free from sin and full of the righteousness of God. I am saved in Jesus name. Amen.*

If you have prayed this prayer to receive Jesus Christ as your personal savior, welcome to your new life of continued victories in God.

# Chapter 3: A Life Ablaze with the Power of God and the Holy Spirit

When the power of God prevails over you, and in you, your life is ablaze with power and the Holy Spirit. Beloved, you are empowered with spiritual audacity. "Greater is He (God) that is within you than he that is in the world." (1 John4:4). When you voice the word of God at any time, you will find that God is greater than any power that is round about you. The enemy (devil) always comes to try you in your weakness, but we should not forget that we are stronger in our weakness than in our strength if we dare believe God's word. It is the only book that has eternal power in every line. Beloved! You must have the word of God abiding in you at all time, and in the most staggering condition of helplessness that you may face in your life. A persistence dose of meditation of the word of God, in the life of a born again believer will produce powerful victorious Christian lives.

Psalm 1:1-3…Blessed is the man who does not walk in the counsel of the wicked or stand in the seat of mockers, but his delight is in the law of the Lord, and on His law he meditates day and night. He is like a tree planted by the streams of water, which yields its fruit in season and whose leaf does not wither. Whatever he does prospers. Beloved like a tree planted, rooted, grounded, secure is a life ablaze with the power of God and thee Holy Spirit. Someone who is unshakable. God wants to create that kind of stable maturity in us and He does it through His word. In his written word, our God reveals His will for our lives (Psalm1:1). But even more important, in His word our God reveals Himself. Knowing God's commands is important;

knowing God is even more important. This kind of knowing involves head, heart, and hands all at once. It transforms our lives and our lifestyle.

We become faith extremes, and radicals because of our unbreakable bond with Him (God). We are able to exercise that gift which God gives us; the ability to trust and see God when others can't. This is what happens when one's life is ablaze with the power of God and the Holy Spirit. This (infilling) always lifts a born again believer to a plane above the ordinary. There is nothing impossible to a born again believer filled with the Holy Spirit. It is beyond all human comprehension. When you are filled with a life ablaze with power of God and the Holy Spirit, God will wonderfully work wherever you go. Beloved, you have no idea what God can do through you when you are filled with His Spirit. Every day and every hour, you have the divine leading of God.

Beloved, the enemy has you as a target of defeat, but God will vindicate you in the midst of the attack.

How important it is that every born again believer be filled with the Holy Spirit. It is the only kind of thing that will enable us to stand. In this life the Lord puts you in all sorts of places and then reveals His power. We have a wonderful gospel and a great Saviour! If you will but be filled with the Holy spirit, you will have a constant spring within; yes, as your faith centers in the Lord Jesus, from within you shall flow rivers of living waters.

The omnipotent power of the Holy is the defense of every contrite soul. No one who in penitence and faith has claimed His protection will Christ permit to pass under the enemy's deceptive ability. The rainbow of promise encircling the throne on high is everlasting testimony that God so loved the world that He gave His only begotten son that who so ever believeth in Him should not perish but have everlasting life. John 3:16. It testifies to the universe that God will never forsake His children in the struggle with evil. It is an assurance to us of strength and protection as long as the throne itself shall endure. As a born again believer whose life is ablaze with the power of the Holy Spirit should look upon the enemy as a conquered foe. You have been given power to tread on serpents and scorpions, over all the power of the enemy and nothing shall by any means hurt you. No weapon formed against you shall prosper. The enemy has deceptive ability to form tragedies and negative consequences in the life of a born again believer. However, you have this anointed, indwelling powerful spirit that will keep you from being overtaken by the enemy.

There is today controversy regarding genuineness of the power of the Holy

Spirit in a born again believer. You will find that God throughout the world has poured our His Spirit in astonishing ways in the midst of His peoples. Our Lord Jesus said to His disciples, "Behold, I send the promise of my father upon you; but tarry ye in the city of Jerusalem until ye be endured with power from on high." (Luke 24:49).

God promised through the prophet Joel, "I will pour out my Spirit upon all flesh... upon the servants and upon the hand maids in those days will I pour out my Spirit."

Beloved, there is more biblical evidence of the baptism of the Holy Spirit. The scriptures will prove my position. In the book of Acts 2:4, they were all filled with the Holy Spirit and began to speak with other tongues as the spirit gave them utterance. Here we have the original pattern. And God gave to Peter an eternal word that couples this experience with the promise that went before: "This is that." And God wants you to have that and nothing less than that. God wants you to receive the baptism in the Holy Spirit according to this original Pentecostal pattern. Beloved, enter into the promises of God. It is your inheritance. Beloved, if you are sure of your ground, if you are counting on the presence of the living Christ within you, you can laugh when you see things getting worse. God would have you settled and grounded in Christ and it is only as you are filled with the Holy Spirit that you become steadfast and unmovable in God. This indwelling divine power of the Holy Spirit. It powers us to be able to resist the temptations that assail us from within and from without. Act in faith and the Lord will meet you every time at the point of your need. Beloved, may God take us on and on into this glorious fact of faith that we may be so directed by the Holy Spirit that God will work through us on the line of the miraculous and on the lines of prophecy where we shall always know that it is no longer we, but He who is working through us bringing forth that which is in His one divine good pleasure.

Something wonderful is going to happen to you!

Study Scriptures on the Holy Spirit

1. Acts - Chapter 2:1-21
2. Romans - Chapter 8:1-17
3. 1 Corinthians - Chapter 2:1-16
4. 1 Corinthians - Chapter 6:12-20
5. 2 Corinthians - Chapter 3:1-6
6. Galatians - Chapter 3:1-14

Beloved, voice your position in God and you will be surrounded by all the resources of God in the time of Trial.

Praise God!

Beloved, repeat in your heart often, "Baptized with the Holy Spirit and fire, fire, fire! All the unction and weeping and travailing comes through the baptism of fire and I say to you and say to myself, purged and cleansed and filled with renewed spiritual power."

The Power of God prevails over you!

# About the Author

Bishop K. R. Simmons, a Pentecostal, Holy Spirit filled servant of God, is the founder of God Ministries of Miracles Temple. He boldly preaches divine healing and the full gospel message to many.

The inner heart and character of this servant of God, his compassion for the unsaved, the sick, and needy. His uncompromising relationship with God who has called and anointed him to lay hands on many. And the power of God rains victorious in the lives of those he touches.

Bishop Simmons realizes that only through the indwelling of the Holy Spirit, he is able to operate in the works of God in this time season.

If this book has changed your life or been a blessing to you, and/or for any prayer request, please write us at:

Bishop K. R. Simmons
God Ministries of Miracles Temple
P. O. Box 20325
Ferndale, MI 48220